Restoring
Coral
Reefs

T0363432

Written by Joshua Hatch

Flying Start
to Literacy®

Contents

Introduction

An animal smaller than a grain of rice can be seen by astronauts in space. How can this be?

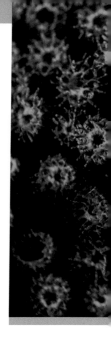

The animal is a coral, and although each one is not much bigger than a sesame seed, they live in colonies with trillions of other corals. Together, they form massive underwater cities called reefs where fish, turtles and many other types of marine life find shelter and live out their lives.

A coral reef is an incredibly important and diverse **ecosystem**. Scientists estimate that a quarter of all marine species live on or around coral reefs. That's even more amazing when you realise coral reefs take up less than 0.1 per cent of the ocean's area. It's also why the destruction of coral reefs is so concerning. Damaging a small patch of ocean where the corals live could wreak havoc on the web of life in the entire ocean and on the earth.

Coral reefs are built from trillions of tiny corals.

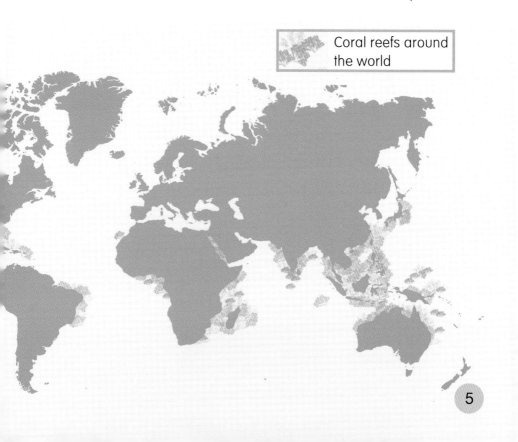

Coral reefs around the world

Chapter 1

An ancient web of life

Some people wrongly think corals are plants, because they look colourful and stay fixed in one location. But they are actually tiny, mostly **transparent** animals that fix themselves to the ocean floor with a shell-like skeleton. Individual corals look a little like miniature upside-down jellyfish. They have small tentacles designed to catch and eat microscopic food floating in the water. So, where do the corals get those amazing colours from?

Plants called algae live inside each coral. The algae are brilliantly coloured, which is why coral reefs look so pretty. These algae turn sunlight into food, which the coral consumes in addition to whatever it filters through the water. In return, the skeleton of the coral gives the algae a safe place to live. Corals and algae live in mutual harmony, each helping the other.

Corals come in many different shapes and colours, but they all have tentacles.

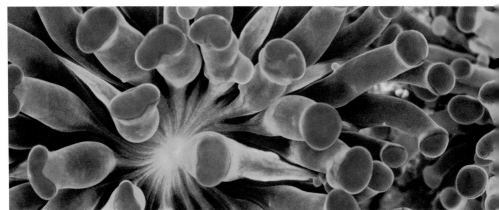

An ancient bond

Corals and algae first formed this bond almost 500 million years ago. But it's only in the last 20,000 years or so that the two have combined to build the giant reefs that dot the planet today.

One of the biggest and best-known reefs is the Great Barrier Reef on the east coast of Australia. On the Great Barrier Reef, there are nearly 6,000 different species of coral, octopi, clams, sponges, worms, fish, jellyfish, sharks, whales, turtles and so much more. Despite the name, the Great Barrier Reef isn't just one single reef, but almost 3,000 reefs! Together, the reefs stretch more than 2,250 kilometres from end to end.

Did you know?
There are more species of fish in a one-hectare patch of healthy coral reef than there are species of birds in North America!

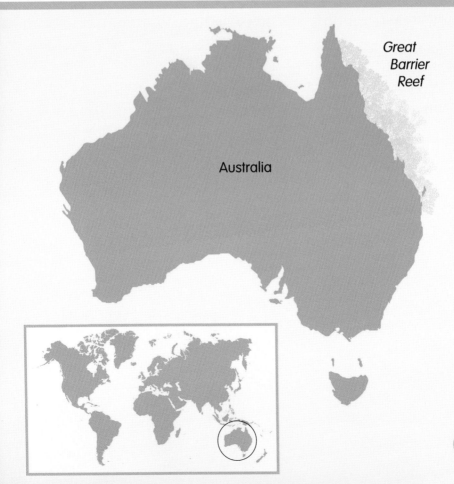

Great Barrier Reef

Australia

A vibrant ecosystem

Reefs are known as the ocean's rainforests because they support a wide variety and large volume of life, like a rainforest on land.

Every part of the reef works together as part of a vibrant **ecosystem**. Reefs, like a forest's trees, are the foundation of the food chain and habitat. Much like a tree gives birds a place to build their nests and raise their young, reefs give fish and other animals holes to hide in and lay eggs.

Reefs are like underwater apartment buildings. Unfortunately, lots of reefs are being damaged or destroyed. And much like knocking down an apartment building would leave many families homeless, the destruction of reefs is leaving lots of marine life without a safe place to live and thrive.

Did you know?
Parrotfish actually eat little pieces of coral. When the fish digest the coral, the pieces break down and come out as sand.

▶ A healthy reef supports a huge range of animals, such as this manta ray and fish.

Chapter 2

Grief along the reef

Coral reefs around the world are in danger. In fact, over the past 30 years, about half the world's reefs have been destroyed.

To understand the various threats coral reefs face, it's critical to understand how fragile and slow growing reefs are. A coral reef grows less than ten centimetres per year. And corals are sensitive to water pollution and water temperature. Most corals can't survive if the water is colder than 22 degrees Celsius or hotter than 28 degrees Celsius.

Climate change

The biggest threat to coral reefs, by far, is climate change. As people pollute the atmosphere with excess carbon dioxide, heat from the sun gets trapped and air temperatures rise. The heat in the air is absorbed by the oceans, warming the water. Over time, the water can heat up to temperatures beyond what the corals can tolerate. The stressed corals **expel** the algae they need to survive. Without the algae, the corals lose their colours and turn bone white – an effect called **coral bleaching**. The corals don't die immediately, but if the bleaching lasts long, or is repeated, the corals cannot survive.

Coral bleaching on the Great Barrier Reef, Australia

13

Storms

Hotter air and water temperatures also increase the frequency and intensity of storms. Cyclones are enormous ocean storms that drive giant, powerful waves through the water. Like wrecking balls knocking down apartment walls, these waves slam into reefs, breaking them and depriving marine life of their homes.

The coral reef at Komodo National Park, Indonesia

Acidification

Too much carbon dioxide in the atmosphere also creates another problem. Seawater absorbs the carbon dioxide, making the water more **acidic** than normal. This is bad for corals because acidic water dissolves their bony skeletons. Just imagine if your skeleton was being dissolved! It's not a good thing.

Storm damage to parts of the coral reef at Komodo National Park, Indonesia

Overfishing

Because reefs are home to so much marine life, it makes sense that they would also be a popular destination for **commercial** fishers. But it's possible to be too popular.

Reefs, like all **ecosystems**, need to live in balance. Fish eat some of the algae that grow with the corals, keeping the algae in check. Overfishing destroys that balance. If too many fish are removed, the algae could grow unchecked and choke off the reef's supply of oxygen and light.

A fishing net lost at sea covers a coral reef.
Fish can get trapped in these nets and die.

Think about it
More than a billion people around the world get their food from the animals that live on or around coral reefs. If those reefs are destroyed, where will those people get their food from?

Blast fishing and bottom trawlers have damaged coral reefs in Malaysia.

Certain types of fishing, especially bottom trawling and blast fishing, can destroy the reef.

Bottom trawlers drag heavy nets across the seafloor, scrubbing away anything growing there. Blast fishing is when explosives are dropped in the water. When they explode, all living creatures are killed and the fish float to the surface. It's hard to imagine a method of fishing more damaging than that!

A crown-of-thorns starfish feeds on a bleached, hard coral on a tropical reef.

Predators

Some threats to coral reefs come from other animals living in the water. One in particular is the crown-of-thorns starfish. It loves to eat coral in an unusual way. This starfish extends its special stomach through its mouth and wraps it around the coral, **liquefying** it.

Typically, this is the natural balance of an ecosystem. But in recent years, huge numbers of crown-of-thorns starfish have been eating corals at an unprecedented rate. As a result, divers in Australia have removed more than 300,000 of these starfish to keep them from destroying the corals more quickly than they can grow.

Other threats

Reefs are also in danger from pollution, disease and human interference. Dumping rubbish, chemicals or other waste into the ocean can smother reefs or foul the water. Dirty water can prevent the algae and corals from growing. Stressed corals become diseased.

And if that's not enough, boaters and divers sometimes break corals, through boating accidents or on purpose to claim souvenirs. None of this is good for the corals; it all contributes to reef and habitat destruction.

Reef damage caused by crown-of-thorns starfish

Chapter 3

Coral nurseries

The outlook for coral reefs is bleak, but not hopeless. Scientists are busy working on methods to protect reefs and help them recover. One approach is to rebuild reefs with new corals raised in **nurseries**.

A group of scientists in Australia is attempting this with corals that survived major bleaching events in 2016 and 2017. The scientists believe that the corals that survived the bleaching events might be better able to cope with warmer and more **acidic** waters in the future.

To grow new corals in the nursery, the scientists take small cuttings from existing reefs. The cuttings are transplanted and cemented to underwater scaffolds. There, the corals grow and reproduce. Just ten cuttings can turn into more than 250 new corals in less than a year!

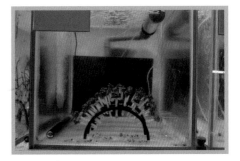

These small pieces of coral are growing in a coral nursery aquarium.

A diver checks the health of coral growing on a scaffold.

Planting corals

After the new corals are big enough, the scientists remove them from the scaffolds and plant them onto the natural reefs. Over time, this process can accelerate reef growth and restore reefs damaged by bleaching.

1 Scientists grow coral fragments in a nursery.

2 When the coral is big enough, it is planted on the reef.

3 Over time, the coral reef grows.

Divers surveying corals growing on a scaffold in the Maldives.

Nurseries need to pick the kinds of coral they want to grow. Some, like staghorn coral, grow quickly but are more likely to break in rough water. Others, like palm and brain coral, are sturdier but take longer to grow.

All these different types of corals are important for a healthy reef. The hope is that nurseries can help reefs recover more quickly than they are destroyed.

Pom Pom Island

On a small island off the coast of Malaysia, a group of volunteers is working to restore a coral reef damaged by war and blast fishing. The Tropical Research and Conservation Centre on Pom Pom Island has replanted more than 75,000 new coral fragments to artificial reef beds. The volunteers also work with local residents to develop more **sustainable** ways to fish and live off the reef.

Pom Pom Island is a small island located off the coast of Sabah, Malaysia.

A volunteer helps cull crown-of-thorns starfish from the reef at Pom Pom Island.

Chapter 4

Saving underwater cities

Protecting and restoring reefs isn't just about saving corals and the animals that live around reefs. Because of climate change caused by humans, the oceans are rising. Warm water is less dense than cold water, so it takes up more space, causing sea levels to rise. Melting glaciers add even more water to the ocean. Warmer air and water create storms that are bigger and stronger – and happen more frequently.

Did you know?
There are different kinds of reefs, but some of the best known are the "barrier" reefs. They get this name because the reef forms a protective barrier between the deep ocean and shallow waters.

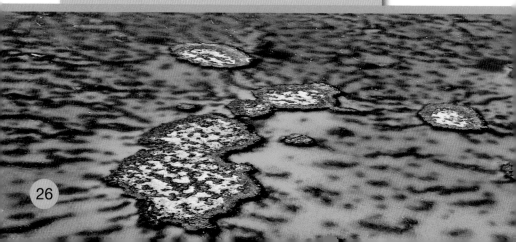

When a major storm develops over the ocean, it pushes water towards the shoreline. Known as a storm surge, this swell of ocean water can flood coasts and wash away beaches, destroying property and killing those who live there.

Coral reefs act like a buffer or sponge, absorbing the energy from the surge and lessening the impact on the coastline. That means reefs are more important than ever to help spread out a cyclone's storm surge and protect coasts from flooding and **erosion**.

Corals help humans

Coral reefs protect people not only from storms but also from disease. Scientists have discovered various chemicals in the corals and surrounding animals that can be turned into drugs to treat a variety of illnesses, from cancer to heart disease to bacterial infections. Who knows what lifesaving compounds could be lurking under the ocean's surface? Or, tragically, what medicines might have existed in a reef that has long since been destroyed?

Reefs also create jobs and support many economies. **Sustainable** fishing feeds hundreds of millions of people. Tourists flock to colourful reefs to snorkel and see the wonders under the waves. It is estimated that nearly $3 trillion a year is generated by people working on and around reefs. That's as much money as the entire economy of France generates each year! And all from a tiny animal that's smaller than a grain of rice plus a single cell of algae – and trillions of their friends.

▲ A coral farm in France. Scientists are interested in the potential of coral chemicals to fight diseases.

▼ A child snorkelling on a coral reef.

Conclusion

The world's coral reefs are in crisis and humans are to blame. If we don't change, most of the world's reefs could be gone by 2050. The good news is that many people are working to solve this problem.

Scientists are working on ways to grow more corals and rebuild reefs. Communities are working to reduce pollution and stop behaviours, like blast fishing, that in minutes can destroy reefs that took thousands of years to grow.

But the biggest step that people can take is to limit climate change. Reducing the emissions of carbon dioxide can slow ocean warming and acidification. Using less energy and switching to renewable sources of energy may be the best ways to ensure coral reefs are here to stay.

Glossary

acidic containing acid, which is a chemical that can break things down

commercial linking to the practice of supplying and selling goods to make money

coral bleaching the result that occurs when the algae that give coral its colour are removed, leaving behind a white skeleton

ecosystem all the animals and plants that depend on one another in a particular area

erosion the process by which something is worn away by wind, water or ice

expel to get rid of

liquefying turning a substance into a liquid so it can be easily digested

nurseries places where young corals can be grown

sustainable linking to a practice that helps make sure something precious isn't used up or destroyed

transparent can be seen through

Index